The Best
ENGLISH
EXERCISES

for
ARABIC
STUDENTS

Beginning
Workbook
One

David Van Ingram

The Best English Exercises for Arabic Students:
Beginning Workbook One
© 2006 by David Van Ingram

David Van Ingram
315 McBrien Road
Chattanooga, Tennessee 37416
USA

Cover design: David Van Ingram and Abdulaziz Al-Rasheed
Text Design: David Van Ingram and Abdulaziz Al-Rasheed

Printed in the United States of America
This book is available online at:

Lulu.com
Amazon.com
Barnesandnoble.com

ISBN Number: 978-1-4357-0823-5

This book is dedicated to
all my students.

David Van Ingram

Acknowledgement

I owe special thanks to Abdulaziz Al-Rasheed and Neil Reynolds for their
moral support and technical assistance in completing this workbook.

Contents

The English Alphabet 1

The English Alphabet: Practice with Lower Case Letters 2

The English Alphabet: Practice with Capital Letters 3

English Vowels 4

a, an 5

Plural Nouns with s and es 6

Plural Nouns: Change y to i and add es 7

Plural Nouns to Memorize 8

Review of Plurals 9

Present Tense: to be 10

Present Tense: contractions of be 11

Present Tense: negative forms of be (contractions) 12

Present Tense: negative forms of be (more contractions) 13

Present Tense: question forms of be 14

There is/There are 15

There is/There are: negatives 16

There is/There are: questions 17

This and *that / these* and *those* 18

Present Tense: to have 19

Present Tense: negative of to have 20

Present Tense: question forms of to have 21

Simple Present Tense 22

Simple Present Tense: negative 23

Simple Present Tense: questions 24

Present Tense: short answers 25

Information Questions 26

More Information Questions 27

Some/Any 28

Imperative Form 29

Possessive Adjectives 30

Object Pronouns 31

Possessive Pronouns 32

Review: Pronouns 33

Let's 34

Present Continuous Tense 35

Present Continuous Tense: negatives 36

v

Present Continuous Tense: questions 37

Past Tense of *be* 38

Past Tense of *be*: negatives 39

Past Tense of *be*: questions 40

Past Tense of Regular Verbs 41

Past Tense of Regular Verbs: negatives 42

Past Tense of Regular Verbs: questions 43

Past Tense of Irregular Verbs 44

Past Tense of Irregular Verbs: negatives 45

Past Tense of Irregular Verbs: questions 46

Common Irregular Verbs in English 47

Future Tense with Going To 48

Future Tense with Going To: negative 49

Future Tense with Going To: questions 50

Must 51

Should 52

May 53

Can and Cannot 54

Review: Questions with Modal Auxiliary Verbs 55

Prepositions 56

More Prepositions 57

Future Tense 58

Future Tense: be 59

Future Tense: negatives 60

Future Tense: simple questions 61

Future Tense: information questions 62

Future Tense: there will be 63

Present Perfect Tense 64

Present Perfect Tense: negative 65

Present Perfect Tense: questions 66

For, Since 67

Already, Yet 68

Present Perfect Continuous Tense 69

Present Perfect Continuous Tense: negatives 70

Present Perfect Continuous Tense: questions 71

Good, Well 72

Adjectives 73

Adjective Opposites 74

Adverbs 75

Adverb Opposites 76

Much, Many 77

A lot of, lots of 78

Have to...79

Have to: negative 80

Have to: questions...81

Have to: past tense 82

Have to: past tense negatives...83

Have to: past tense questions 84

Have to: future 85

Have to: future negative...86

Have to: future questions 87

Have to: present perfect...88

Have to: present perfect negatives 89

Have to: present perfect questions 90

Reflexive Pronouns..91

Reflexive Pronouns: *by oneself* 92

Perfect Modals: *should have*...93

Perfect Modals: *ought to have*...94

Perfect Modals: *could have* 95

Perfect Modals: *may have*..96

Perfect Modals: *might have* 97

Perfect Modals: *must have*...98

Continuous Modals...99

Be supposed to..100

Preface

I began teaching English when I was a Peace Corps Volunteer in the Sultanate of Oman in the 1980s. My experiences in Oman provided a very positive introduction to Arabia and to teaching, so I returned and taught English in the region for many years.

My experience and my observations over the years have led me to compile this workbook. The exercises will be useful to the student on his or her step-by-step journey to learn English vocabulary and grammar.

David Van Ingram

Riyadh, Saudi Arabia
October 2006

The English Alphabet

There are twenty-six letters in the English alphabet.

a b c d e f g h i j k l m n o p q r s t u v w x y z

Exercise: Practice writing each letter on the lines below, like this:

a	b	c	d	e	f	g	h	i	j
1	2	3	4	5	6	7	8	9	10
k	l	m	n	o	p	q	r	s	t
11	12	13	14	15	16	17	18	19	20
u	v	w	x	y	z				
21	22	23	24	25	26				

Practice

1	2	3	4	5	6	7	8	9	10
11	12	13	14	15	16	17	18	19	20
21	22	23	24	25	26				

1

The English Alphabet: Practice Writing the Lower Case Letters

1.   a _____ _____ _____ _____ _____

2.   b _____ _____ _____ _____ _____

3.   c _____ _____ _____ _____ _____

4.   d _____ _____ _____ _____ _____

5.   e _____ _____ _____ _____ _____

6.   f _____ _____ _____ _____ _____

7.   g _____ _____ _____ _____ _____

8.   h _____ _____ _____ _____ _____

9.   i _____ _____ _____ _____ _____

10. j _____ _____ _____ _____ _____

11. k _____ _____ _____ _____ _____

12. l _____ _____ _____ _____ _____

13. m _____ _____ _____ _____ _____

14. n _____ _____ _____ _____ _____

15. o _____ _____ _____ _____ _____

16. p _____ _____ _____ _____ _____

17. q _____ _____ _____ _____ _____

18. r _____ _____ _____ _____ _____

19. s _____ _____ _____ _____ _____

20. t _____ _____ _____ _____ _____

21. u _____ _____ _____ _____ _____

22. v _____ _____ _____ _____ _____

23. w _____ _____ _____ _____ _____

24. x _____ _____ _____ _____ _____

25. y _____ _____ _____ _____ _____

26. z _____ _____ _____ _____ _____

2

The English Alphabet: Practice Writing the Capital Letters

1. _A_ ___ ___ ___ ___ ___
2. _B_ ___ ___ ___ ___ ___
3. _C_ ___ ___ ___ ___ ___
4. _D_ ___ ___ ___ ___ ___
5. _E_ ___ ___ ___ ___ ___
6. _F_ ___ ___ ___ ___ ___
7. _G_ ___ ___ ___ ___ ___
8. _H_ ___ ___ ___ ___ ___
9. _I_ ___ ___ ___ ___ ___
10. _J_ ___ ___ ___ ___ ___
11. _K_ ___ ___ ___ ___ ___
12. _L_ ___ ___ ___ ___ ___
13. _M_ ___ ___ ___ ___ ___
14. _N_ ___ ___ ___ ___ ___
15. _O_ ___ ___ ___ ___ ___
16. _P_ ___ ___ ___ ___ ___
17. _Q_ ___ ___ ___ ___ ___
18. _R_ ___ ___ ___ ___ ___
19. _S_ ___ ___ ___ ___ ___
20. _T_ ___ ___ ___ ___ ___
21. _U_ ___ ___ ___ ___ ___
22. _V_ ___ ___ ___ ___ ___
23. _W_ ___ ___ ___ ___ ___
24. _X_ ___ ___ ___ ___ ___
25. _Y_ ___ ___ ___ ___ ___
26. _Z_ ___ ___ ___ ___ ___

3

English Vowels

a b c d e f g h i j k l m n o p q r s t u v w x y z

Five of the English letters are used in a special way in English. They are called vowels. These letters are a, e, i, o, u. All the other letters are called consonants.

Exercise: Write the English vowels on the lines below:

____   ____   ____   ____   ____

Exercise: Study the words below. See how each vowel has two sounds: a *short* sound and a *long* sound.

Short Vowel Sounds	Long Vowel Sounds
a as in *cat*	*a* as in *ape*
e as in *egg*	*e* as in *me*
i as in *ink*	*i* as in *ice*
o as in *olive*	*o* as in *open*
u as in *us*	*u* as in *useful*

Exercise: Decide if the initial vowels are *short* or *long*. Write the word in the correct list below.

	Short Vowel	Long Vowel
ape	egg	ape
egg		
internet		
orange		
university		
uncle		
apple		
island		
olive		
ice		
email		
ode		

4

a, an

an is used before a word that begins with a **vowel sound**.

a is used before a word that begins with a consonant sound.

an umbrella (umbrella begins with the short u vowel sound, ŭ)
a universe (universe begins with a long u, which has a consonant sound like y)

an apricot	a boy
an uncle	a university
an honor	a hair
an unusual color	a European car
an only child	a one-time chance

Exercise: Place *a* or *an* before the words below:

1. ___a___ good job

2. ___an___ apple pie

3. _____ hair brush

4. _____ horror movie

5. _____ honorable man

6. _____ earthquake

7. _____ one-day trip

8. _____ eggplant

9. _____ orbit

10. _____ used car

11. _____ history lesson

12. _____ artichoke

13. _____ television

14. _____ ice cube

15. _____ ink pen

16. _____ U.S. ship

17. _____ unicorn

18. _____ unit

Plural Nouns with s and es

To make most nouns plural, an s is placed at the end of the word.

pencil---pencils   desk---desks   book---books

Add **es** to nouns that end in s, sh, ch, z, or x.

bus---bus**es**   glass---glass**es**   wish---wish**es**
watch---watch**es**   buzz---buzz**es**   fox---fox**es**

Exercise: Form the plurals of the nouns below by adding *s* or *es*.

1. grass   _____
2. table   _____
3. hat   _____
4. dress   _____
5. notebook   _____
6. fax   _____
7. dish   _____
8. paper   _____
9. plant   _____
10. box   _____

11. friend   _____
12. uncle   _____
13. watch   _____
14. lunch   _____
15. eye   _____
16. class   _____
17. adz   _____
18. door   _____
19. boss   _____
20. problem   _____

6

Plural Nouns: Change y to i and add es

Some nouns end with *y* and have a vowel (*a*, *e*, *i*, *o*, or *u*) before the *y*. In this case just add *s*.

toy---toys   monkey---monkeys   donkey---donkeys

However, if the letter before the *y* is a consonant, the *y* is changed to *i* and then *es* is added to the end of the word.

one fami*ly*---two famil*ies*   one f*ly*--some fl*ies*
one dictiona*ry*---many dictionar*ies*

Exercise: Write the plural form of each word below.

1. brother   _brothers_   11. friend   _____
2. sister   _____   12. uncle   _____
3. family   _____   13. lady   _____
4. boy   _____   14. diary   _____
5. key   _____   15. eye   _____
6. book   _____   16. country   _____
7. city   _____   17. candy   _____
8. father   _____   18. play   _____
9. mother   _____   19. pony   _____
10. refinery   _____   20. dictionary _____

Plural Nouns to Memorize

1. A few nouns have irregular plurals that must be memorized.

deer---deer	goose---geese	mouse---mice
man---men	woman---women	child---children
tooth---teeth	foot---feet	ox---oxen

2. A noun that ends in **f** or **fe** changes its ending to **ves**.

leaf--lea**ves**   wife--wi**ves**   loaf--loa**ves**

3. Nouns that end in **o** with a consonant before the **o** end with **es**.

potat**o**--potat**oes**   her**o**--her**oes**   tomat**o**--tomat**oes**

Exercise: Write the plural form of the nouns below.

1. man   _men_ _____

2. hero   _____

3. shelf   _____

4. knife   _____

5. woman   _____

6. tooth   _____

7. goose   _____

8. mouse   _____

9. foot   _____

10. child   _____

Review of Plurals

Exercise: Write the plural forms of the singular nouns below.

1. box _____
2. grass _____
3. table _____
4. hat _____
5. dress _____
6. notebook _____
7. fax _____
8. dish _____
9. paper _____
10. plant _____
11. friend _____
12. uncle _____
13. watch _____
14. lunch _____
15. eye _____
16. class _____
17. door _____
18. boss _____
19. problem _____
20. brother _____
21. sister _____
22. family _____
23. boy _____
24. key _____
25. fly _____

26. book _____
27. city _____
28. father _____
29. mother _____
30. refinery _____
31. lady _____
32. diary _____
33. candy _____
34. play _____
35. pony _____
36. dictionary _____
37. man _____
38. hero _____
39. shelf _____
40. knife _____
41. woman _____
42. tooth _____
43. goose _____
44. mouse _____
45. foot _____
46. child _____
47. leaf _____
48. tomato _____
49. desk _____
50. ox _____

Present Tense: to be

I **am**
you **are**
he **is**
she **is**
it **is**
we **are**
you **are**
they **are**

Exercise: Practice writing forms of the verb *to be* on the lines below.

1. I ___*am*___ a student.

2. We _____ students.

3. Abdulla _____ a teacher.

4. She _____ a doctor.

5. It _____ a cat.

6. We _____ friends.

7. You students _____ busy.

8. Khalid _____ a tall boy.

9. Yousif and I _____ athletes.

10. Sami _____ an engineer.

11. Layla _____ a nurse.

12. Mishmish _____ a cat.

13. Ali and I _____ brothers.

14. You and your father _____ busy.

Present Tense: contractions of be

Subject + verb	Contraction
I am	I'm
you are	you're
he is	he's
she is	she's
it is	it's
we are	we're
you are	you're
they are	they're

Exercise: Practice writing contractions of the verb *to be* on the lines below.

1. (I am) _____I'm_____ a student.

2. (We are)_____ students.

3. (John is)_____ a teacher.

4. (She is)_____ a doctor.

5. (It is) _____ a cat.

6. (We are) _____ friends.

7. (You are) _____ busy.

8. (They are) _____ at school.

9. (I am) _____ a clerk.

10. (You and I are)_____ friends.

11. (Abdulla is)_____ a teacher.

12. (She is) _____ a dentist.

13. (It is) _____ a cat.

14. (We are) _____ cousins.

15. (You workers are) _____ busy.

16. (They are) _____ at work.

11

Present Tense: negative forms of *be*

Subject + be + not	Subject + Contraction
I am not	*I'm not*
you are not	*you're not*
he is not	*he's not*
she is not	*she's not*
it is not	*it's not*
we are not	*we're not*
you are not	*you're not*
they are not	*they're not*

Exercise: Practice writing the negative of the verb *to be* on the lines below.

1. They are early.
   not/late

   They are not late.

   They're not late.

2. You are busy.
   not/sleepy

3. We are friends.
   not/brothers

4. We are students.
   not/engineers

5. Ahmed is a geologist.
   not/a teacher

6. Huda is a pharmacist.
   not/ a doctor

7. I am a student.
   not/a teacher

Present Tense: negative forms of *be*

Subject + be + not	Subject + Contraction
I am not	(no contraction)
you are not	you aren't
he is not	he isn't
she is not	she isn't
it is not	it isn't
we are not	we aren't
you are not	you aren't
they are not	they aren't

Exercise: Practice writing the negative of the verb *to be* on the lines below.

1. They are early.
   not/late

   <u>They are not late.</u>
   <u>They aren't late.</u>

2. You are busy.
   not/sleepy

3. We are friends.
   not/brothers

4. We are students.
   not/engineers

5. Ahmed is a geologist.
   not/a teacher

6. Huda is a pharmacist.
   not/ a doctor

7. I am a student.
   not/a teacher

13

Present Tense: question forms of *to be*

To make a question with *to be*, place the verb before the subject. Notice the use of the question mark.

Am I?
Are you?
Is he?
Is she?
Is it?
Are we?
Are you?
Are they?

Exercise: Practice making questions with *to be* on the lines below.

1. ___Am___ I a teacher?

2. _____ we engineers?

3. _____ Ahmed a geologist?

4. _____ Huda a doctor?

5. _____ it a cat or a rabbit?

6. _____ we friends?

7. _____ you busy?

8. _____ they at home?

9. _____ I a dentist?

10. _____ they engineers?

11. _____ she a geologist?

12. _____ Salwa a doctor?

13. _____ it a sheep or a goat?

14. _____ you brothers?

15. _____ you and your friend busy?

16. _____ they at work?

14

There is/there are

There is or *there are* is used to show that something is in a certain place. *There is* is used for singular nouns; *there are* is used for plural nouns.

Singular	**Plural**
There is a bird in the tree.	There are birds in the tree.

Exercise: Complete the following sentences with *There is* or *There are.*

1. <u>There is</u> someone on the telephone for you.

2. _____ a lot of employees in this company.

3. _____ one cafeteria in this building.

4. _____ a lot of English classes in this building.

5. _____ four oceans in the world.

6. _____ nobody left in the office.

7. _____ only one key to this lock.

8. _____ many clouds in the sky.

9. _____ only one tree in the garden.

10. _____ a test in English today.

There is/there are: negatives

The negative forms of *there is* and *there are* are made by putting *not* after the verb. The contracted forms *isn't* and *aren't* are often used.

Singular	Plural
There is a bird in the tree.	There are birds in the tree.
There is not a bird in the tree.	There are not birds in the tree.
There isn't a bird in the tree.	There aren't birds in the tree.

Exercise: Change the sentences below from affirmative to negative.

Use the contractions *There isn't* or *There aren't*.

1. There is a full moon in the sky.
    There isn't a full moon in the sky.

2. There are two buildings in that town.
    _____

3. There is a famous city in every country.
    _____

4. There is a police officer on each corner.
    _____

5. There are many hospitals in the area.
    _____

6. There are enough desks for everybody.
    _____

7. There is a Chinese restaurant near here.
    _____

8. There are twenty-five students in this room.
    _____

9. There is a large cloud of dust over the city.
    _____

10. There is a large cloud of dust over the city.
    _____

16

There is/there are: questions

Form questions with *there is* and *there are* by putting the verb before *there*. End the sentence with a question mark.

Singular	**Plural**
There is a bird in the tree.	There are birds in the tree.
Is there a bird in the tree?	Are there birds in the tree?

Exercise: Change the following sentences to questions.

1. There is a full moon in the sky.
   Is there a full moon in the sky?

2. There are two tall buildings on that road.

   _____

3. There is a capital city in each country.

   _____

4. There is a police officer on each corner.

   _____

5. There are several hospitals in the area.

   _____

6. There are enough desks for everybody.

   _____

7. There is a Chinese restaurant near here.

   _____

8. There are twenty-five students in this room.

   _____

9. There is a large cloud of dust over the city.

   _____

10. There are a lot of rivers in Arabia.

    _____

This and that / these and those

This indicates that something is near. That indicates that something is not near. Both this and that are used as pronouns--and as adjectives.

These is the plural of **this**. **Those** is the plural of **that**.

This is a desk.	That is a chalkboard.
This house is Tamer's house.	That house over there is Sami's house.
These desks are empty.	Hilal and Majid sit in those desks.
These houses are empty.	Tamer and Sami live in those houses.

Exercise: In the sentences below, change the singular form to the plural form. Change other parts of the sentence as needed.

1. This hotel is new. _These hotels are new._

2. That computer belongs to Nadir. _____

3. That man is an excellent teacher. _____

4. This lesson is not difficult. _____

5. This fax is for you. _____

6. This email is for Leyla. _____

7. That is my brother. _____

8. This is my sister. _____

9. That cat is my cat. _____

10. This dog is not my dog. _____

11. This pen belongs to Moza. _____

12. That pencil belongs to Saeed. _____

18

Present Tense: *to have*

I **have**
you **have**
he **has**
she **has**
it **has**
you **have**
we **have**
they **have**

Exercise: Practice using the verb *to have* on the lines below.

1. I _____have_____ a new book.

2. We _____ new books.

3. He _____ a very good computer.

4. She _____ a laptop.

5. It _____ food in its dish.

6. We _____ work to do.

7. You _____ a lot to learn.

8. Nawwaf_____ a new car.

9. Huda and Nabeel _____ new books.

10. Noor _____ a very good computer.

11. Farida _____ a laptop.

12. Mishmish_____ water in his bowl.

13. The dentist_____ work to do.

14. They _____ a lot of homework.

Present Tense: negative of *to have*

Do not and *does not* before the verb have forms the negative.
The contractions don't and doesn't are also used.

I ***do not have***	I ***don't*** have
you ***do not have***	you ***don't*** have
he ***does not have***	he ***doesn't*** have
she ***does not have***	she ***doesn't*** have
it ***does not have***	it ***doesn't*** have
we ***do not have***	we ***don't*** have
you ***do not have***	you ***don't*** have
they ***do not have***	they ***don't*** have

Exercise: Practice using the negative of the verb *to have* on the lines below.

1. I _____*don't have*_____ a new book. I have an old book.

2. We _____ new books. We have old books.

3. He _____ a very good computer. He has his father's old computer.

4. She _____ a laptop computer. She has a desktop computer.

5. The cat is hungry. It _____ food in its dish.

6. We have work to do. We _____ time for a coffee break.

7. You have a lot to learn. You _____ a lot of experience.

20

Present Tense: question forms of *to have*

Use *do* or *does* before the subject to make questions with *have*.
Complete the question with a question mark.

I have	*Do I have?*
you have	*Do you have?*
he have	*Does he have?*
she has	*Does she have?*
it has	*Does it have?*
we have	*Do we have?*
you have	*Do you have?*
they have	*Do they have?*

Exercise: Practice making questions with *have* on the lines below. End each
sentence with a question mark.

1. I have a new book. (you) ___Do you have___ a new book too?

2. We have new books. (they) _____ new books too __

3. He has a very good computer. (he) _____ a laptop __

4. She has a laptop computer. (she) _____ a desktop computer also __

5. The cat doesn't have food in its dish. (it) _____ water in its bowl __

6. We have a lot of work to do. (we) _____ time for a coffee break __

7. You have a lot to learn. (you) _____ a plan to study in college __

Simple Present Tense

The simple present tense describes an action which goes on every day or in general. In the third person singular (he, she, it), *s* is added to the verb.

I **walk**
you **walk**
he **walks**
she **walks**
it **walks**
we **walk**
you **walk**
they **walk**

Exercise: Practice using simple present tense verbs in the sentences below.

1. (walk) I __walk__ five kilometers every day.

2. (work) We _____ for a company in Riyadh.

3. (know) He _____ how to repair computers.

4. (use) She _____ a laptop computer.

5. (eat) It _____ the food in its dish.

6. (drive) We _____ to work every day.

7. (learn) You _____ a lot when you visit other countries.

Simple Present Tense: negative

The simple present tense describes an action which goes on every day or in general. In the third person singular (he, she, it), *s* is added to the verb. To negate a present tense verb, **not** is used with the helping verb *do (don't)*. *He, she*, and *it* require *doesn't*.

I **walk**	I **do not walk**	I **don't walk**
you **walk**	you **do not walk**	you **don't walk**
he walks	he **does not walk**	he **doesn't walk**
she walks	she **does not walk**	she **doesn't walk**
it walks	it **does not walk**	it **doesn't walk**
we **walk**	we **do not walk**	we **don't walk**
you **walk**	you **do not walk**	you **don't walk**
they **walk**	they **do not walk**	they **don't walk**

Exercise: Practice using simple present tense verbs in the sentences below. Write the negative forms *don't* and *doesn't*.

1. I walk to the shop every day. I __*don't*__ drive to the shop.

2. We work for a company in Riyadh. We_____ work in Houston.

3. He knows how to repair computers. He _____know how to write software.

4. She uses a laptop computer. She _____ own a desktop computer.

5. The cat eats the food in its dish. It _____ eat the rabbit's food.

6. We drive to work every day. We _____ take the bus.

7. Some people _____ like to travel.

23

Simple Present Tense: questions

Do or *does* begins the present tense question. Except for *be*, almost all verbs use *do/does* as an auxiliary verb in simple present tense questions. *Do/does* has no meaning in these questions.

Do I walk?
Do you walk?
Does he walk?
Does she walk?
Does it walk?
Do we walk?
Do you walk?
Do they walk?

Exercise: Form simple present tense questions from these statements.

1. I walk five kilometers every day.

   Do I walk five kilometers every day?

2. We work for a company in Riyadh.

   _____

3. He knows how to repair computers.

   _____

4. She uses a laptop computer.

   _____

5. It eats the food in its dish.

   _____

6. We drive to work every day.

   _____

Present Tense: short answers

Short answers are given to direct questions. A subject and an auxiliary verb forms a short answer

Are you happy?	Yes, **I** am.	No, **I'm** not.
Does he work?	Yes, **he** does.	No, **he** doesn't.
Can she read?	Yes, **she** can.	No, **she** can't.

Exercise: Use short answers to say *yes* to the questions below.

1. Am I happy?
   Yes, I am.
2. Is this your book?

3. Are you hungry?

4. Can you speak English?

5. Does your teacher speak Arabic?

6. Is today Saturday?

7. Are you from Riyadh?

8. Is the weather nice today?

9. Can you drive a car?

10. Can you play computer games?

11. Do you play computer games?

12. Am I your friend?

13. Are you my friend?

14. Is Rajeh our friend?

15. Do you like dates?

16. Does it rain in Salalah?

17. Is Jeddah a beautiful city?

18. Can you visit Dubai?

Exercise: Use short answers to say *no* to the questions above.

25

Information Questions

A present tense question is formed by using a question word and putting do or does before the subject of the sentence. Information questions begin with question words like *who, where, when, what* and how.

Exercise: Fill in the blanks below with the correct form, *do* or *does*.

1. Where _____does_____ Amir live?

2. How often _____ you go to Bahrain?

3. What time _____ the plane leave for Doha?

4. How many languages _____ you speak?

5. When _____ you get up in the morning?

6. Where _____ you usually meet your friends after school?

7. How long _____ your lesson last?

8. How _____ you feel today?

9. Why _____ you want to save your money?

10. How often _____ you go to the park?

More Information Questions

Information questions begin with information words like *where, when, what,* and *how.*

where	to ask about location
when	to ask about time
what	to ask general questions
how	to ask about quality or characteristics

Exercise: Use the word in parentheses to begin an information question.

1. They live in Jubail. (Where)
   Where do they live?

2. They travel by bus. (How)

3. It rains in April. (When)

4. The lesson begins at eight o'clock. (What time)

5. The books belong on the bookshelf. (Where)

6. The book belongs on the bookshelf. (Where)

7. He feels fine. (How)

8. They eat lunch in the cafeteria. (Where)

9. I go to bed at ten o'clock. (What time)

10. These books cost fifty riyals. (How much)

11. He drives a Toyota. (What kind of)

12. He visits once a week. (How often)

Some/Any

Some is used in statements that are affirmative.
There are **some** yellow flowers in that garden.

Any is used in statements that are negative.
There aren't **any** yellow flowers in that garden.

Exercise: Choose the correct answer. Write your answers on the blank lines.

1. There are (some, any) comfortable chairs in that room. _____some_____
2. There aren't (some, any) boys in the park. _____
3. There aren't (some, any) homework questions to do. _____
4. There are (some, any) people coming to the party. _____
5. I see (some, any) stars in the sky. _____
6. I don't see (some, any). _____
7. I learn (some, any) new words every day. _____
8. He makes (some, any) mistakes in spelling. _____
9. She never makes (some, any) mistakes in grammar. _____
10. I don't give Misfer (some, any) money. _____
11. I don't have (some, any) money in my pocket. _____
12. I have (some, any) money in my wallet. _____
13. There are (some, any) people downtown tonight. _____
14. There aren't (some, any) people in the park. _____
15. I see (some, any) people near the corniche. _____
16. I don't see (some, any) people in the water. _____
17. I have (some, any) work to do on Thursday. _____
18. I buy (some, any) fruit at the market on Thursday. _____
19. I don't buy (some, any) vegetables. _____
20. We have (some, any) visitors coming on Friday. _____

Imperative Form

When you make a command or a request, you can use the imperative form. In statements using the imperative form, the subject is understood to be *you*. Negative imperatives use *don't*.

Answer the phone, please.   *(You) answer the phone, please.*
Look in the mirror.   *(You) look in the mirror.*
Don't move.   *(You) don't move.*

Exercise: Change the sentences below using the negative imperative form.

1. Wait for me.   *Don't wait for me.*

2. Look out the window.   _____

3. Drive your car fast.   _____

4. Speak Arabic in the lesson.   _____

5. Close the window.   _____

6. Open the door.   _____

7. Come back after lunch.   _____

8. Do your homework in the classroom.   _____

9. Be angry.   _____

10. Forget what I told you.   _____

11. Come to work tomorrow.   _____

12. Leave the classroom early.   _____

13. Let him see you.   _____

14. Borrow money.   _____

15. Eat a lot of chocolate.   _____

Possessive Adjective

Possessive adjectives are placed in front of a noun to modify it and to show possession. The possessive adjectives are **my**, **your**, **his**, **her**, **its**, **your**, **our** and **their**. Each must agree in gender and number with the owner, not the noun.

Elizabeth does **her** homework.
Phillip brushes **his** teeth.
They wash **their** car.

Exercise: Complete the sentences below with a correct possessive adjective.

1. **He** does _____ *his* homework every evening.

2. **I** also do _____ homework every evening.

3. **You** always eat _____ lunch quickly.

4. *Reza* drives to work in _____ car.

5. *Hamza and I* enjoy _____ English class.

6. Each *cat* has _____ own dish.

7. Do *you* like _____ English teacher?

8. We rode with *Fatima* in _____ car.

9. We saw *Sarah* at _____ house.

10. *She* invited us to _____ house for tea.

30

Object Pronouns

Subject Pronouns	Object Pronouns
I	me
you	you
he	him
she	her
it	it
we	us
you	you
they	them

Direct objects, indirect objects, and objects of prepositions are object pronouns.

Mother gave it to *her*.
Dad gave *him* a pen.
He taught English to *us*.

Exercise: Replace the underlined noun with a pronoun form.

1. He sells tea to <u>*Nasser*</u> everyday.
   He sells tea to *him* everyday.

2. She gives milk to <u>*the cat*</u> every morning.

3. They do homework with <u>*Fawwaz and Jamal*</u> each evening.

4. I know <u>*Aloush*</u> very well.

5. Mother usually makes cakes for <u>*the children*</u>.

6. Husain has dinner with <u>*John and me*</u>.

7. We work with <u>*Hala*</u> at the clinic.

8. I know him and <u>*his sister*</u>.

9. Mother and Father often buy <u>*toys*</u> for the baby.

10. She and I always eat lunch with <u>*Huda and Leyla*</u>.

31

Possessive Pronouns

The possessive pronouns in English are:

mine

yours

his

hers

ours

theirs

Exercise: Complete the sentences below with a correct possessive pronoun.

1. This book is _my book_. This book is _mine._

2. These are _her pens_. These are _hers._

3. These pencils are _his pencils_. These are _____.

4. Those books are _my books_. Those are _____.

5. Is all of this money _your money_? Is all of this _____?

6. The big house with the beautiful garden is _their house_. It is _____.

7. Is this your cell phone or _Mr. Reynold's cell phone_? Is it _____.?

8. Is that _her car_? Is that _____?

9. Bob's shirt and _my shirt_ are very similar. Bob's shirt is similar to _____.

10. Their car is the same color as _our car_. It's the same color as _____.

Review
Subject Pronouns, Object Pronouns, Possessive Adjectives and Posessive Pronouns

Subject Pronoun	Object Pronoun	Posessive Adjective	Possessive Pronoun
I	Me	my	mine
you	You	your	yours
he	Him	his	his
she	Her	her	hers
it	It	its	its
we	Us	our	ours
you	You	your	yours
they	Them	their	Theirs

Exercise: Fill in the blanks below with the correct pronoun or possessive adjective listed above.

I have a car.	The car belongs to _____.	It is _____ car.	It is _____.
You own a house.	The house belongs to _____.	It is _____ house.	It is _____.
He has a shop.	The shop belongs to _____.	It is _____ shop.	It is _____.
She has a garden.	The garden belongs to _____.	It is _____ garden.	It is _____.
It has a mouse.	The mouse belongs to _____.	It is _____ mouse.	It is _____.
We own a farm.	The farm belongs to _____.	It is _____ farm.	It is _____.
You own a company.	The company belongs to_____.	It is____ company.	It is _____.
They have a boat.	The boat belongs to _____.	It is _____ boat.	It is _____.

Let's

Suggestions in English often begin with **let's** *(let us)*.
The negative form of *let's* is ***let's not***.

Let's go out for dinner tonight.
Let's not go out for dinner tonight.

Exercise: Change the imperative statements below to suggestions. Use *let's*.
Write the negative form of the statement using *let's not*.

1. Call Hamoody tonight.
   Let's call Hamoody tonight.
   Let's not call Hamoody tonight.

2. Take the test this afternoon.
   _____
   _____

3. Watch the movie on the DVD.
   _____
   _____

4. Go to the park.
   _____
   _____

5. Take our vacations together.
   _____
   _____

Present Continuous Tense

Use the present continuous tense to describe what is happening *now*. Verbs in the present continuous tense are formed by using the simple present form of *be* (*am*, *is*, or *are*) and *ing* at the end of the verb:

Subject	+ be	+ verb	+ ing
I	am	teach	ing
He	is	study	ing
We	are	read	ing

I am teaching.
He is studying.
We are reading.

Exercise: Rewrite the sentences below using a present continuous form of the verb in each sentence.

1. I (study) the new lesson.
   _____I am studying the new lesson._____

2. He (read) a book.
   _____

3. She (talk) on the telephone.
   _____

4. You (listen) to the teacher.
   _____

5. We (learn) English.
   _____

6. You (watch) television.
   _____

7. They (cook) dinner.
   _____

8. Ali (wash) his car.
   _____

9. Huda (write) a letter.
   _____

10. Nabeel and Ali (play) a computer game.
    _____

Present Continuous Tense: Negative

To form the negative of the present continuous tense, place **not** between the helping verb and the main verb:

> I am **not** teaching.
> He is **not** studying.
> We are **not** reading.

Exercise: Write a meaningful sentence below using the negative form of the present continuous tense.

1. I am studying. (not teach)

   I am not teaching.

2. He is playing a computer game. (not study)

   _____

3. We are writing letters. (not reading)

   _____

4. She is doing her homework. (not talk on phone)

   _____

5. They are looking at the new house. (not buy)

   _____

6. You are listening to music. (not watch TV)

   _____

7. Huda is cooking dinner. (not eat)

   _____

8. Ali is driving his car. (not wash)

   _____

Present Continuous Tense: Questions

To form a question in the present continuous tense, place a form of the helping verb **be** (*am*, *is*, or *are*) at the beginning of the sentence. Use a question mark at the end of the sentence.

Am I teaching?
Is he studying?
Are we reading?

Exercise: Read the answers below. Write an appropriate question using the present continuous tense. Don't forget to use a question mark.

1. *Are you doing your homework?*
   No, I am not doing my homework. I am writing a letter.

2. _____
   No, Mother is not making lunch. She is cooking dinner.

3. _____
   No, he isn't checking his email. He is browsing the internet.

4. _____
   No, they're not watching TV. They're listening to music.

5. _____
   No, I am not teaching English. I am studying English.

6. _____
   No, Nabeel isn't taking a shower. He's brushing his teeth.

7. _____
   No, Aloush isn't washing his car. He's waxing it.

8. _____
   No, they're not moving out of that house. They are moving in.

9. _____
   No, we're not buying a house. We're buying an apartment.

10. _____
    No, you aren't studying French. You're studying English.

37

Past Tense of *be*

Present Tense	Past Tense
I am	I was
you are	you were
he is	he was
she is	she was
it is	it was
we are	we were
you are	you were
they are	they were

Exercise: Rewrite each sentence in the past tense.

1. He is a good worker. _____He was a good worker._____.

2. I am a good worker too. _____.

3. Hamza is busy. _____.

4. This grammar lesson is easy. _____.

5. Aloush and I are good friends. _____.

6. Nabeel is a good friend. _____.

7. The door is locked. _____.

8. Majid and Husain are new teachers. _____.

9. I am an experienced teacher. _____.

10. He is an experienced teacher. _____.

11. You are a good student. _____.

12. You are good students. _____.

38

Past Tense of be: negative

Present Tense	Past Tense
I am not	I was not (I wasn't)
you are not (you aren't)	you were not (you weren't)
he is not (he isn't)	he was not (he wasn't)
she is not (she isn't)	she was not (she wasn't)
it is not (it isn't)	it was not (it wasn't)
we are not (we aren't)	we were not (we weren't)
you are not (you aren't)	you were not (you weren't)
they are not (they aren't)	they were not (they weren't)

Exercise: Rewrite the sentences below. Use the negative past tense of *be*.

1. He was a good worker. _He wasn't a good worker._ .

2. I was a good worker too. _____.

3. Hamza was busy. _____.

4. This grammar lesson was easy. _____.

5. Aloush and I were good friends. _____.

6. Nabeel was a good friend. _____.

7. The door was locked. _____.

8. Majid and Husain were new teachers. _____.

9. I was an experienced teacher. _____.

10. He was an experienced teacher. _____.

11. You were a good student. _____.

12. You were good students. _____.

Past Tense of be: questions

Present Tense Questions	Past Tense Questions
Am I not?	Was I not? (Wasn't I?)
Are you not? (Aren't you?)	Were you not? (Weren't you?)
Is he not? (Isn't he?)	Was he not? (Wasn't he?)
Is she not? (Isn't she?)	Was she not? (Wasn't she?)
Is it not? (Isn't it?)	Was it not? (Wasn't it?)
Are we not? (Aren't we?)	Were we not? (Weren't we?)
Are you not? (Aren't you?)	Were you not? (Weren't you?)
Are they not? (Aren't they?)	Were they not? (Weren't they?)

Exercise: Make questions from the sentences below. Use the past tense of *be*.

1. He was a good worker. _Was he a good worker?_ .

2. I was a good worker too. _____.

3. Hamza was busy. _____.

4. This grammar lesson was easy. _____.

5. Aloush and I were good friends. _____.

6. Nabeel was a good friend. _____.

7. The door was locked. _____.

8. Majid and Husain were new teachers. _____.

9. I was an experienced teacher. _____.

10. He was an experienced teacher. _____.

11. You were a good student. _____.

12. You were good students. _____.

40

Past Tense of Regular Verbs

The past tense of regular verbs is formed by adding *-ed* to the present tense form.

walk	walked
talk	talked
work	worked
like	liked
want	wanted
need	needed
fix	fixed
repair	repaired

Present Tense	**Past Tense**
I *walk* to work every day.	I *walked* to work yesterday.

Exercise: Write sentences using the past tense of the regular verbs.

1. (walk) For exercise, we <u>walked</u> five kilometers every day.

2. (talk) I _____ to Majed on the phone last night.

3. (work) Huda _____ an extra hour yesterday afternoon.

4. (like) The children _____ the cakes Mother made for them.

5. (want) Fawwaz's father _____ to teach him how to drive.

6. (need) Rashid _____ a pencil to write his homework.

7. (fix) The mechanic _____ Ahmed's car last week.

8. (repair) Ahmed's brother Ramadan _____ his own car.

Past Tense of Regular Verbs: negatives

The negative past tense of regular verbs is formed by adding *did not* (didn't) before the present tense form of the verb.

walked	did not walk (didn't walk)
talked	did not talk (didn't talk)
worked	did not work (didn't work)
liked	did not like (didn't like)
wanted	did not want (didn't want)
needed	did not need (didn't need)
fixed	did not fix (didn't fix)
repaired	did not repair (didn't repair)

<u>Past Tense</u>	<u>Negative Past Tense</u>
I *walked* to work.	I did not *walk* to work.

Exercise: Write sentences using the negative past tense of the regular verbs.

1. I talked to Majed on the phone last night.
   I didn't talk to Majed on the phone last night.

2. Huda worked an extra hour yesterday.
   _____

3. The children liked the cakes Mother made for them.
   _____

4. Fawwaz's father wanted to teach him how to drive.
   _____

5. Rashid needed a pencil to write his homework.
   _____

6. The mechanic fixed Ahmed's car last week.
   _____

Past Tense of Regular Verbs: questions

Questions made with the past tense of regular verbs are formed by placing *did* at the beginning of the sentence and a question mark at the end.

Present Tense Statement
He walked to work.

Past Tense Question
Did he walk to work?

Exercise: Make past tense questions from the statements below.

1. I talked to Majed on the phone last night.
   Did I talk to Majed on the phone last night?

2. Huda worked an extra hour yesterday.

   _____

3. The children liked the cakes Mother made for them.

   _____

4. Fawwaz's father wanted to teach him how to drive.

   _____

5. Rashid needed a pencil to write his homework.

   _____

6. The mechanic fixed Ahmed's car last week.

   _____

7. Leyla repaired her own computer.

   _____

8. Mother washed our clothes yesterday.

   _____

43

Past Tense of Irregular Verbs

Irregular verb forms do not follow a pattern when they change, so these verbs must be memorized. Here are a few examples.

Present Tense	Past Tense
go	went
see	saw
teach	taught
write	wrote
read	read
sit	sat
stand	stood
hurt	hurt

Exercise: Complete the sentences with the past tense form of the verb.

1. My mother ___went___ to Paris last year.
   (go)

2. I _____ a nice watch in that shop.
   (see)

3. She _____ us English for five years.
   (teach)

4. Aloush _____ his homework in his notebook.
   (write)

5. Ali _____ in that desk yesterday.
   (sit)

6. The teacher _____ in front of the students.
   (stand)

44

Past Tense of Irregular Verbs: negative

Past Tense	Negative Past Tense
went	didn't go
bought	didn't buy
taught	didn't teach
wrote	didn't write
sat	didn't sit
stood	didn't stand

The negative past tense is formed by placing *did not* (*didn't*) in front of the simple form of the verb.

I *went* to work today. (I *didn't* go to work today.)

Exercise: Rewrite the sentences below to make them negative.

1. I went to Paris with my mother.
   I didn't go to Paris with my mother.

2. I bought the nice watch.

   _____

3. She taught us French.

   _____

4. He always wrote his homework in his notebook.

   _____

5. He sat in that desk last week.

   _____

6. The teacher always stands when he teaches.

   _____

Past Tense of Irregular Verbs: questions

To make questions in the past tense, use *did* before the subject and use the simple form of the verb.

Did I go to work today?
Did you go to work today?
Did he go to work today?
Did she go to work today?
Did it go to work today?
Did you go to work today?
Did we go to work today?
Did they go to work today?

Exercise: Read the answers below. Then, write an appropriate question in the past tense.

1. _Did you go with your mother to Paris?_
   Yes, I did. I went with her to Paris.

2. _____
   Yes, I did. In fact, I bought two watches.

3. _____
   Yes, we did. We enjoyed studying French.

4. _____
   No, he didn't. He didn't do his homework.

5. _____
   No, you didn't. You sat in that chair last week.

6. _____
   No, he didn't. He sat at his desk during the lesson.

Common Irregular Verbs in English

Present	Past	Past Participle	Present	Past	Past Participle
am/is/are	was/were	been	leave	left	left
beat	beat	beaten	lend	lent	lent
become	became	become	let	let	let
begin	began	begun	lie	lay	lain
bend	bent	bent	lose	lost	lost
bite	bit	bitten	make	made	made
blow	blew	blown	mean	meant	meant
break	broke	broken	meet	met	met
bring	brought	brought	pay	paid	paid
build	built	built	put	put	put
burst	burst	burst	read	read	read
buy	bought	bought	ride	rode	ridden
catch	caught	caught	ring	rang	rung
choose	chose	chosen	rise	rose	risen
come	came	come	run	ran	run
cost	cost	cost	say	said	said
deal	dealt	dealt	sell	sold	sold
dig	dug	dug	send	sent	sent
do	did	done	shake	shook	shaken
draw	drew	drawn	shoot	shot	shot
drink	drank	drunk	show	showed	shown
drive	drove	driven	shut	shut	shut
eat	ate	eaten	sit	sat	sat
fall	fell	fallen	sleep	slept	slept
feed	fed	fed	speak	spoke	spoken
feel	felt	felt	spend	spent	spent
fight	fought	fought	split	split	split
find	found	found	spread	spread	spread
fly	flew	flown	stand	stood	stood
forbid	forbade	forbidden	steal	stole	stolen
forget	forgot	forgotten	stick	stuck	stuck
forgive	forgave	forgiven	sting	stung	stung
freeze	froze	frozen	strike	struck	struck
get	got	gotten	swear	swore	sworn
give	gave	given	sweep	swept	swept
go	went	gone	swim	swam	swum
grow	grew	grown	swing	swung	swung
hang	hung	hung	take	took	taken
have	had	had	teach	taught	taught
hear	heard	heard	tear	tore	torn
hide	hid	hidden	tell	told	told
hit	hit	hit	think	thought	thought
hold	held	held	throw	threw	thrown
hurt	hurt	hurt	understand	understood	understood
keep	kept	kept	wake	woke	woken
know	knew	known	wear	wore	worn
lay	laid	laid	win	won	won

47

Future Tense with *Going to*

Going to expresses a planned future action and is formed this way:

subject + be + going + infinitive
I am going to watch TV.
You are going to watch TV.
He is going to watch TV.
She is going to watch TV.
It is going to watch TV.
You are going to watch TV.
We are going to watch TV.
They are going to watch TV.

Exercise: Change the sentences below to future tense with *going to.*

1. I will go to college when I finish high school.
    <u>I am going to go to college when I finish high school.</u>

2. He studies English.
    _____

3. We ate dinner at our friend's house.
    _____

4. She is sixteen years old.
    _____

5. It is waiting for you.
    _____

6. There will be an exam on Wednesday.
    _____

7. They're playing football.
    _____

8. You bought some new clothes.
    _____

9. Everybody bring something to the picnic.
    _____

10. We will go to the mountains for the weekend.
    _____

48

Future Tense with *Going to*: negative

The negative of *going to* uses *not* after *be*, and is formed this way:

subject + be +not + going + infinitive

I am not going to watch TV.
You are not going to watch TV.
He is not going to watch TV.
She is not going to watch TV.
It is not going to watch TV.
You are not going to watch TV.
We are not going to watch TV.
They are not going to watch TV.

Exercise: Make the sentences below negative.

1. He is going to study English.
   He is not going to study English. (He isn't going to study English).

2. We are going to eat dinner at our friend's house.

   _____

3. She is going to be sixteen years old.

   _____

4. It is going to wait for you.

   _____

5. There is going to be an exam on Wednesday.

   _____

6. They're going to play football.

   _____

7. You are going to buy some new clothes.

   _____

8. Everybody is going to bring something to the picnic.

   _____

Future Tense with *Going to*: questions

Questions with *going to* are formed this way:
<u>*be + subject + going + infinitive +?*</u>

Am I going to watch TV?
Are you going to watch TV?
Is he going to watch TV?
Is she going to watch TV?
Is it going to watch TV?
Are you going to watch TV?
Are we going to watch TV?
Are they going to watch TV?

Exercise: Make questions for the answers below.

1. Are you going out tonight?
   _____

   Yes, I am. I am going to go out tonight.

2. _____

   No, they're not. They're not going to go shopping.

3. _____

   Now we aren't. We aren't going to buy a new house this year.

4. _____

   Yes, she is. She is going to buy a new car.

5. _____

   No, they aren't. They aren't going to go out for dinner tonight.

6. _____

   Yes, they are. They are going to bring all the food for the picnic.

7. _____

   Yes, we are. We are going to go to Malaysia next year.

8. _____

   No it isn't. It isn't going to be cold tomorrow.

Must

Must is a modal auxiliary verb that is used with a main verb to convey obligation. The negative is formed by placing *not* after must and is usually contracted to *mustn't*.

The students must *go to lunch early.*
The students must not *go to lunch early.*
The students mustn't *go to lunch early.*

Exercise: Change the sentences below to the negative. First use ***must not***. Write the sentence again with ***mustn't***.

1. I must wait here.
   _____ I must not wait here. _____
   _____ I mustn't wait here. _____

2. She must cook spaghetti today.
   _____
   _____

3. It must enter the house.
   _____
   _____

4. They must come tomorrow at this time.
   _____
   _____

5. We must tell Aloush about the meeting.
   _____
   _____

6. You must open the window immediately.
   _____
   _____

7. He must return on Saturday to his father's house.
   _____
   _____

8. Huda must spend the money her mother gave her.
   _____
   _____

Should

Should is a modal auxiliary verb that is used with a main verb to recommend or advise. The negative is should not or shouldn't.

You should *learn to speak English in England.*
You should not *learn to speak English in Spain.*
You shouldn't *learn to speak English in Spain.*

Exercise: Change the sentences below to the negative. First use **should not**. Write the sentence again with **shouldn't**.

1. I should work seven days a week.
   I should not work seven days a week.
   I shouldn't work seven days a week.

2. He should speak Italian in this class.
   _____
   _____

3. She should tell her sister everything.
   _____
   _____

4. It should stay outside the house.
   _____
   _____

5. You should draw that picture again.
   _____
   _____

6. We should sit next to the window.
   _____
   _____

7. They should buy another car.
   _____
   _____

8. We should talk during the lesson.
   _____
   _____

May

May is used to ask for and to give permission. The negative *may not* <u>denies</u> permission.

> May *I use your car?*
> *Yes, you* may. *You* may *use my car today.*
> *You* may not *use my car tomorrow.*

Questions beginning with *may* are most often, but not always, in the first person. *May I /May we* means *do you allow me to?*

> *May I* **use your car?**
> *May we* **use your car?**

Exercise: Write questions with *may* for the answers below.

1. <u>May I come with you?</u>
   Yes, you may. You may come with us.

2. _____
   Yes, of course you may wait here. This is a waiting room.

3. _____
   Yes, you may. Both of you may sit here.

4. _____
   No, you may not. You may not smoke here.

5. _____
   No, you may not. You may not sleep on the floor.

6. _____
   No, you may not. You may not use the telephone.

Can and Cannot

Can is a modal auxiliary verb that means *able to do*. In the question form, it is used to ask permission.

I *can* **come at eight o'clock.**
Can **I come at eight o'clock?**
Yes, you *can.*

The negative of can is can+not, or *cannot*. It is written as one word.

Can **I come at eight o'clock?**
No, you *cannot.*

Exercise: Make a question from the statements below, then answer the question with a negative short answer using cannot. Finally, write a complete negative statement using cannot.

1. He can sing beautifully.
   Can he sing beautifully? No, he cannot.
   He cannot sing beautifully.

2. She can carry the heavy box.
   _____
   _____

3. They can meet them later.
   _____
   _____

4. We can call them later.
   _____
   _____

5. She can make delicious cakes.
   _____
   _____

6. We can take the course again.
   _____
   _____

Review: Questions with Modal Auxiliary Verbs

Exercise: Change the statements to questions.

1. He can speak Spanish well.

   Can he speak Spanish well?

2. We should wait outside.

   _____

3. You may have coffee.

   _____

4. She must attend the meeting.

   _____

5. You should tell Aloush about it.

   _____

6. Huda should stay at home.

   _____

7. Nabeel can meet us after dinner.

   _____

8. They can swim very well.

   _____

9. We can attend the class tomorrow.

   _____

10. I can finish my homework.

    _____

11. You may rent the house for a year.

    _____

Prepositions

Prepositions indicate location or direction. Here is a list of common prepositions.

in	on	above	in front of	in back of
with	by	over	of	next
beside	under	at	for	to

Exercise: Use the prepositions above to complete the sentences below.

1. I usually walk_____to_____ work.

2. He likes sugar _____ his tea.

3. She put the book _____ the table.

4. The map is _____ the wall _____ the teacher's desk.

5. Our teacher stands _____ us.

6. The chalkboard is _____ our teacher.

7. We go_____ the cafeteria _____ our friends.

8. They like to go_____ Dammam _____ train.

9. The horse jumped _____ the fence.

10. Hot is the opposite _____ cold.

11. My best friend, Aloush, sits _____in class.

12. She parks her car _____ the house _____ a tree.

13. I usually arrive _____ seven o'clock.

14. They thanked them _____the gift.

15. We put the stamp _____the envelope.

56

More Prepositions

Here is another list of common prepositions.

about	against	instead of	without	in back of
across	after	ahead	along	among
aside	between	opposite	on top of	outside

Exercise: Complete the sentences below with the correct preposition.

1. He thinks ____*about*____ going to London all the time.

2. The children should go _____ and play.

3. The manager lives _____ the street from me.

4. My house is _____ the manager's house.

5. The street _____ our houses is called Azalea Lane.

6. You are working _____ a group of very nice people.

7. He took me _____ and advised me to come to work on time.

8. The students are _____ increasing the tuition.

9. I got an apartment just _____ the supermarket.

10. Ahmed walked _____ the Nile and watched the fishing boats.

11. I found the lost door key _____ the tall cabinet.

12. I prefer to eat French fries _____ ketchup.

13. You should always keep looking _____ when you are driving.

14. I would rather have bread _____ rice with the roast chicken.

15. Let's have coffee _____ dinner, if you don't mind.

57

Future Tense

The auxiliary verb **will** is used with a simple verb to form the future tense. Contractions are generally used.

Subject+will+verb	Contraction
I will study	I'll study
you will study	you'll study
he will study	he'll study
she will study	she'll study
it will study	it'll study
we will study	we'll study
you will study	you'll study
they will study	they'll study

Exercise: Change the sentences to the future tense. Write the complete verb. Then write the sentence again using the contraction won't.

1. I work in that company.
   I will work in that company.
   I'll work in that company.

2. He speaks English well.
   _____
   _____

3. She comes to the lesson on time.
   _____
   _____

4. It happens soon.
   _____
   _____

5. You study at the library.
   _____
   _____

6. They travel by train.
   _____
   _____

Future Tense: be

The future form of be is *will be*. Contractions are normally used.

Subject+will+verb	Contraction
I will be home	*I'll be* home
you will be home	*you'll be* home
he will be home	*he'll be* home
she will be home	*she'll be* home
it will be home	*it'll be* home
you will be home	*you'll be* home
we will be home	*we'll be* home
they will be home	*they'll be* home

Exercise: Change the sentences below to the future tense. Write the complete verb. Then, write the sentence again using a contraction.

1. I am in the library.

   I will be in the library.

   I'll be in the library.

2. They are in the classroom.

   _____

   _____

3. He is your new teacher.

   _____

   _____

4. It is on the table.

   _____

   _____

5. You are in Riyadh.

   _____

   _____

6. I am in Jeddah.

   _____

   _____

Future Tense: negative

The negative future tense is formed by placing *will not (won't)* in front of the simple form of the verb.

Subject+will+not+verb	**Subject+contraction+verb**
I *will not* drive.	I *won't* drive.
You *will not* drive.	You *won't* drive.
He *will not* drive.	He *won't* drive.
She *will not* drive.	She *won't* drive.
It *will not* drive.	It *won't* drive.
You *will not* drive.	You *won't* drive.
We *will not* drive.	We *won't* drive.
They *will not* drive.	They *won't* drive.

Exercise: Change the sentences below to the negative. Write the complete verb. Then, write the sentence again using the contraction won't.

1. He will walk to work.
   <u>He will not walk to work.</u>
   <u>He won't walk to work.</u>

2. She will come to the lesson on time.
   _____
   _____

3. It will happen soon.
   _____
   _____

4. You will study at the library.
   _____
   _____

5. They will travel by train.
   _____
   _____

6. We will go with them.
   _____
   _____

Future Tense: simple questions

Simple questions in the future tense begin with *will* followed by a subject and a verb.

Will I go to work today?
Will you go to work today?
Will he go to work today?
Will she go to work today?
Will it go to work today?
Will you go to work today?
Will we go to work today?
Will they go to work today?

Exercise: Change the statements below to future tense questions.

1. I will buy a new car next month.
Will you buy a new car next month?

2. He will move to the new job next week.
_____

3. She will plan her wedding for December.
_____

4. It will be the largest shopping center in the area.
_____

5. You will see big changes.
_____

6. We will take a vacation in the summer.
_____

7. They will build a new house next year.
_____

8. We will miss him when he goes.
_____

9. Those people will come for dinner.
_____

10. You will get a promotion next month.
_____

61

Future Tense: information questions

Information questions in the future tense begin with a question word in front of *will*, followed by a subject and a verb.

When will I go to work today?
How will you go to work today?
What time will he wake up?
Where will she go?
What will it do?
Who will you visit?
Why will we arrive late?

Exercise: Change the statements below to future information questions.

1. I will buy a new car next month.
   When will you buy a new car?

2. He will move to the new job next week.
   _____

3. She will plan her wedding this summer.
   _____

4. You will see big changes next year.
   _____

5. We will take a vacation in the summer.
   _____

6. They will build a new house next year.
   _____

7. Those people will come for dinner at eight.
   _____

8. He will succeed in the course by working hard.
   _____

9. You will get a promotion next month.
   _____

10. All of the staff members will be coming for the meeting.
   _____

Future Tense: there will be

The future forms of *there is and there are* is *there will be.*
There is treated like a subject in future statements and questions.

There will be a quiz on Wednesday.
Will there be a quiz on Wednesday?

Exercise: Change the statements below to questions.

1. There will be a meeting tomorrow morning.
    Will there be a meeting tomorrow morning?

2. There will be coffee and donuts at the meeting.

    _____

3. There will be a party this Thursday night.

    _____

4. There will be a football match on Friday.

    _____

5. There will be a dinner at our house.

    _____

6. There will be a lot of people there.

    _____

7. There will be another chance to get a promotion.

    _____

8. There will be a change in the weather.

    _____

9. There will be many opportunities as the company grows.

    _____

10. There will be gifts for everyone.

    _____

Present Perfect Tense

The present perfect tense is formed with *have* or *has* and the past participle of a verb (see the list of past participles on page 47).

I have learned
you have learned
he has learned
she has learned
it has learned
you have learned
we have learned
they have learned

Compare the present perfect tense to the simple past tense.

Past tense: *Ahmed **learned** the English alphabet last Saturday.*
Present perfect: *Huda **has learned** a lot of English grammar rules.*

The simple past tense happens at a definite time in the past (last Saturday). The present perfect tense refers to past action where the exact moment of the action is uncertain.

Exercise: Write the verbs in the present perfect tense.

1. She (take) me there many times.   _She has taken me there many times._

2. He (finish) his homework.   _____

3. They (go) to Jeddah many times   _____

4. We (learn) a lot of English grammar.   _____

5. We (drive) to Dhahran many times.   _____

6. I (lose) a hundred riyals.   _____

7. She (make) cakes for everyone.   _____

8. You (help) me a lot with my homework.   _____

64

Present Perfect Tense: negative

The negative of the present perfect tense is formed by placing *not* after *have* or *has*. The contraction is *haven't*.

I have not learned	I haven't learned
you have not learned	you haven't learned
he has not learned	he hasn't learned
she has not learned	she hasn't learned
it has not learned	it hasn't learned
you have not learned	you haven't learned
we have not learned	we haven't learned
they have not learned	they haven't learned

Exercise: Change the sentences to the negative present perfect tense.

1. She has taken me there.   *She hasn't taken me there.* _____

2. He has finished his homework. _____

3. They have gone to Jeddah. _____

4. We have learned a lot of English grammar. _____

5. We have driven to Dhahran. _____

6. I have lost a hundred riyals. _____

7. She has made cakes for everyone. _____

8. You have helped me a lot. _____

9. John has taught English to many students. _____

10. I have read that book three times. _____

11. I have seen that movie twice. _____

12. He has lent me money several times. _____

13. The loud noise has given me a headache. _____

14. That teacher has been here for many years. _____

Present Perfect Tense: questions

Questions in the present perfect tense are formed by beginning the question with *have* or *has*.

Have I seen it?
Have you seen it?
Has he seen it?
Has she seen it?
Has it seen it?
Have you seen it?
Have we seen it?
Have they seen it?

Exercise: Change the sentences to present perfect tense questions.

1. She has taken me there. _Has she taken me there?_
2. He has finished his homework. _____
3. They have gone to Jeddah. _____
4. We have learned a lot of English grammar. _____
5. We have driven to Dhahran. _____
6. I have lost a hundred riyals. _____
7. She has made cakes for everyone. _____
8. You have helped me a lot. _____
9. John has taught English to many students. _____
10. I have read that book three times. _____
11. I have seen that movie twice. _____
12. He has lent me money several times. _____
13. The loud noise has given me a headache. _____
14. That teacher has been here many years. _____

For, Since

For and *since* are often used with the present perfect tense. *For* is used to indicate a period of time; *since* is used to indicate a specific point in time.

I have worked here **for** *five years.*

I have worked here **since** *2003.*

Exercise: Complete the sentences below with *for* or *since*.

1. I have taught English ____for____ many years.

2. He has studied English _____ he was five years old.

3. She has studied math _____ she moved to Riyadh.

4. He has studied Spanish _____ three years.

5. You have lived here _____ you were born.

6. Your parents have lived here _____ twenty years.

7. They have been teachers _____ they graduated.

8. They have been teachers _____ seven years.

9. The cat has not eaten _____ we left.

10. It has waited _____ eight hours.

Already, Yet

Already and *yet* are often used with the present perfect tense. *Already* is used as an affirmative. It means *by this time or earlier*. *Yet* is used in negative statements.

I have **already** *eaten lunch.*

I have not eaten lunch **yet.**

Exercise: Complete the sentences below with *already* or *yet*.

1. We aren't hungry. We have <u>already</u> eaten.

2. The children are hungry. They haven't eaten _____.

3. Ahmed has _____ left for the airport.

4. They have not arrived home _____.

5. I haven't paid the electric bill _____.

6. I have _____ received my salary.

7. I haven't accepted the new job _____.

8. I have not moved out of my apartment _____.

9. We have _____ bought a house.

10. We haven't moved into the house _____.

Present Perfect Continuous: questions

Questions in the present perfect continuous tense begin with *have* or *has*.

Have I been studying?
Have you been studying?
Has he been studying?
Has she been studying?
Has it been studying?
Have we been studying?
Have you been studying?
Have they been studying?

Exercise: Change the statements below to questions.

1. I have been teaching English for ten years.

   Have I been teaching English for ten years?

2. He has been studying English since he was five years old.

   _____

3. She has been studying math since she moved to Riyadh.

   _____

4. He has been studying Spanish for three years.

   _____

5. You have been living here since you were born.

   _____

6. Your parents have been living here for twenty years.

   _____

7. It has been waiting for eight hours.

   _____

Present Perfect Continuous: negatives

The negative form of the present perfect continuous tense is formed with *have not been* (haven't been) or *has not been* (hasn't been) and the present participle of the main verb.

I *have not been studying.*   I *haven't been studying.*
You *have not been studying.*   You *haven't been studying.*
He *has not been studying.*   He *hasn't been studying.*
She *has not been studying.*   She *hasn't been studying.*
It *has not been studying.*   It *hasn't been studying.*
We *have not been studying.*   We *haven't been studying.*
You *have not been studying.*   You *haven't been studying.*
They *have not been studying.*   They *haven't been studying.*

Exercise: Change the sentences below to the negative.

1.   I have been teaching English for many years.
     I haven't been teaching English for many years.

2.   He has been studying English since he was five years old.
     _____

3.   She has been studying math since she moved to Riyadh.
     _____

4.   He has been studying Spanish for three years.
     _____

5.   You have been living here since you were born.
     _____

6.   Your parents have been living here for twenty years.
     _____

7.   It has been waiting for eight hours.
     _____

Present Perfect Continuous: questions

Questions in the present perfect continuous tense begin with *have* or *has.*

Have I been studying?
Have you been studying?
Has he been studying?
Has she been studying?
Has it been studying?
Have we been studying?
Have you been studying?
Have they been studying?

Exercise: Change the statements below to questions.

1. I have been teaching English for ten years.
    Have I been teaching English for ten years?

2. He has been studying English since he was five years old.
    _____

3. She has been studying math since she moved to Riyadh.
    _____

4. He has been studying Spanish for three years.
    _____

5. You have been living here since you were born.
    _____

6. Your parents have been living here for twenty years.
    _____

7. It has been waiting for eight hours.
    _____

Good, Well

An adjective is a word that describes a noun. An adjective can come before or after the noun it describes. When it comes after the noun, it is preceded by a form of be.

Good is an adjective:

This is good ice cream. Or, *This ice cream is good.*

Well is an adjective when it describes someone's health:

You look well today.

Otherwise, *well* is an adverb. An adverb describes the action of a verb. Adverbs normally come after the verb they describe:

He speaks English well.

(Well describes how *he speaks.)*

Exercise: Complete the sentences below with the adjective *good* or the adverb *well*.

1. Ahmed plays football ____well____.

2. She is a _____ student.

3. They are _____ teachers.

4. They teach _____.

5. This is a _____ brand of mobile phone.

6. It really works _____.

7. My mother cooks _____.

8. She makes _____ food.

9. The weather today is _____.

10. You look _____. Did you just come from vacation?

72

Adjectives

An adjective describes a noun. Adjectives generally have three forms.

basic adjective	comparative	the superlative
cold	colder than	the cold**est**
hot	hotter than	the hot**test**
big	bigger than	the bigg**est**
fast	faster than	the fast**est**
sweet	sweeter than	the sweet**est**
good	better than	the best
bad	worse than	the worst

Most adjectives follow a pattern. The comparative is formed by adding **-er** to the basic adjective and is used with *than*. The superlative is formed by adding **-est** to the basic adjective and preceding it with *the*. Irregular adjective forms like *good* and *bad* must be memorized.

Exercise: Complete the sentences below with the best adjective in the proper form.

1. November is a cold month, but December is __colder than__ November.
2. January is _____ month.
3. May is a hot month, but June is _____ May.
4. July is _____ month.
5. Mexico is a big country, but the United States is_____ Mexico.
6. In North America, Canada is _____ country.
7. A rabbit is fast, but a gazelle is _____ a rabbit.
8. A cheetah is _____ animal on earth.
9. Sugar is sweet, but maple syrup is _____ sugar.
10. Honey is _____ food in nature.

Adjective Opposites

An adjective describes a noun. Study the adjectives and their opposite meanings below.

good	bad
hot	cold
sweet	sour
light	dark
happy	sad
big	little
large	small
deep	shallow

Exercise: Complete the sentences below with the best adjective.

1. I am smiling and _____ today.

2. I usually feel happy. I don't often feel _____.

3. In July the weather is _____.

4. In January the weather can be _____.

5. The sky during the day is _____ blue.

6. The sky at night can be _____ blue.

7. Hamoody is a _____ boy. He is 5 years old.

8. Nasser is a _____ boy. He is seventeen years old.

9. The Gulf is _____.

10. The Red Sea is _____.

11. When I am happy, I feel _____.

12. When I am sad, I feel _____.

Adverbs

An adverb describes the action of a verb. Adverbs generally have three forms.

basic adverb	comparative	the superlative
fast	faster than	the fastest
hard	harder than	the hardest
slowly	more slowly than	the slowest
neatly	more neatly than	the neatest
completely	more completely than	the most completely
well	better than	the best
bad	worse than	the worst

The comparative of a one-syllable adverb is formed by adding **-er** to the basic adverb and is used with *than*. The superlative is formed by adding **–est** to the basic adjective and preceding it with *the*. Irregular adverb forms like *well* and *bad* must be memorized.

Exercise: Complete the sentences below with the best adverb in the proper form.

1. Ahmed runs fast, but Aloush runs _____*faster than*_____ Ahmed.

2. Abdulaziz runs _____*the fastest*_____ .

3. Huda works hard, but Reem works _____ Huda.

4. Huda and Reem's mother works _____ .

5. A rabbit runs fast, but a gazelle runs _____ a rabbit.

6. A cheetah runs _____ .

7. Sugar tastes sweet, but corn syrup tastes _____ sugar.

8. Honey tastes _____

9. John did well on the test, but Elizabeth did _____ John.

10. Phillip made the highest score. He did _____ .

Adverb Opposites

An adverb describes the action of a verb. Study the adverbs and their opposites below.

fast	slowly
hard	softly
slowly	quickly
lightly	heavily
completely	slightly
well	badly
equally	unequally

Exercise: Complete the sentences below with the best adverb.

1. Rajeh drives _____.

2. Huda drives _____.

3. Yasser hit the ball _____.

4. She spoke _____ into her mother's ear.

5. Majed was _____ surprised by his birthday party.

6. Fortunately, they were only _____ hurt in the car accident.

7. She speaks English _____.

8. He writes English _____.

9. She divided the cake _____ into twelve pieces.

10. Money is _____ divided between the rich and the poor.

Much, Many

Use *much* with nouns that cannot be counted and do not form plurals with *s*.

much coffee	much rice
much time	much milk
much love	much juice

Use *many* with nouns that can be counted and can be made plural with *s*.

many cups of coffee	many bags of rice
many visits	many cows
many feelings	many oranges

Exercise: Complete the sentences below with *much* or *many*.

1. I don't spend __much__ time on my homework.

2. You have _____ friends.

3. Does he spend _____ money on food?

4. This company has _____ good employees.

5. This town has _____ good people.

6. There are _____ mountains in Oman.

7. How _____ time do you spend studying?

8. How _____ times have you traveled to Jeddah?

9. We don't have _____ money.

10. They don't have _____ children.

A lot of, lots of

A lot of and *lots of* have exactly the same meaning. Both phrases replace much or many.

much coffee	a lot of coffee
much time	a lot of time
much love	a lot of love
much coffee	lots of coffee
much time	lots of time
much love	lots of love

Exercise: Replace *much* or *many* in the sentences below with *a lot of and lots of.*

1. I don't spend much time on my homework.
    I don't spend ____a lot of___ time on my homework.
    I don't spend ____lots of___ time on my homework.
2. You have many friends.
    You have _____ friends.
    You have _____ friends.
3. Does he spend much money on food?
    Does he spend _____ money on food?
    Does he spend _____ money on food?
4. This company has many good employees.
    This company has _____ good employees
    This company has _____ good employees
5. This town has many good people.
    This town has _____ good people.
    This town has _____ good people.
6. There are many mountains in Oman.
    There are _____ mountains in Oman.
    There are _____ mountains in Oman.
7. We don't have much money.
    We don't have _____ money.
    We don't have _____ money.

Have to

Have to has the same meaning as the modal *must,* whichexpresses need or duty.

I **must** get a key made.	I **have** to get a key made.
You **must** get a key made.	You **have** to get a key made.
He **must** get a key made.	He **has** to get a key made.
She **must** get a key made.	She **has** to get a key made.
It **must** get a key made.	It **has** to get a key made.
You **must** get a key made.	You **have** to get a key made
We **must** get a key made.	We **have** to get a key made.
They **must** get a key made.	They **have** to get a key made.

Exercise: Rewrite the sentence below. Use a form of *have to.*

1. I must go to lunch soon.   *I have to go to lunch soon.*
2. I must get up early in the morning _____
3. You must have more money.   _____
4. She must finish her homework.   _____
5. I must go to the dentist.   _____
6. We must send them more money.   _____
7. They must leave for Paris tonight. _____
8. It must eat once a day.   _____
9. Ahmed must find a new job.   _____
10. Elizabeth must wait for them.   _____

Have to: negative (don't have to)

The negative of *have to* is *don't have to* or *doesn't have to*.
Don't have to means that there is no obligation or necessity to do something.

There is no need to worry.	I don't have to worry.
You shouldn't worry	You don't have to worry.
He mustn't worry.	He doesn't have to worry.
She needn't worry.	She doesn't have to worry.
It mustn't worry.	It doesn't have to worry.
Don't worry.	You don't have to worry.
We mustn't worry.	We don't have to worry.
They shouldn't worry.	They don't have to worry.

Exercise: Change the sentences to don't have to or doesn't have to.

1. I need not go to work on Thursday.
   You don't have to go to work on Thursday.

2. There is no need for him to go to the bank tomorrow.
   _____

3. She shouldn't worry about cooking dinner tonight.
   _____

4. It need not wait for its food.
   _____

5. You will have enough time. Don't worry.
   _____

6. We needn't prepare lesson plans on Friday.
   _____

7. They shouldn't worry about money. Their father is rich.
   _____

8. There is no work tomorrow. You needn't get up early.
   _____

9. Aloush can stay at our house tonight. He needn't go home.
   _____

10. Huda shouldn't worry about cooking. Mother cooks for her.
    _____

Have to: questions

Questions with *have to* begin with *do* or *does.*

Do you have to go home?   Does he have to live with his parents?

Exercise: Make question forms from the statements below. Use *do...have to* or *does...have to.*

1. I must go to lunch soon.   <u>Do you have to go to lunch soon?</u>

2. I must get up early in the morning. _____

3. You must have more money.   _____

4. She must finish her homework.   _____

5. I must go to the dentist.   _____

6. We must send them more money.   _____

7. They must leave for Paris tonight. _____

8. It must eat once a day.   _____

9. Ahmed must find a new job.   _____

10. Elizabeth must wait for them.   _____

81

Have to: past tense

Had to is the past tense of *have to/has to*. It expresses need or duty in the past.

He *had to* stay with his parents while they were ill.
We *had to* move to another city to find jobs.
They *had to* buy a new car when their old one stopped running.

Exercise: Change the sentences below to the past tense. Use *had to*.

1. I have to be on time for the meeting.
   I had to be on time for the meeting.

2. You have to finish your homework.
   _____

3. He has to give me more money.
   _____

4. They have to wait for the train.
   _____

5. She has to sell her jewelry.
   _____

6. All the students have to take the test.
   _____

7. You have to read the instructions again.
   _____

8. We have to sleep on the floor.
   _____

9. Aloush has to find a new apartment.
   _____

10. Huda has to ask her mother for money.
    _____

Have to: past tense negatives

The past tense of *had to* is *didn't have to*.
He *didn't have to* teach on Thursdays.
We didn't have to do any homework.
They didn't have to show their ID cards.

Exercise: Change the sentences below to the negative past tense. Use *didn't have to*.

1. I have to be on time for the meeting.
   <u>I didn't have to be on time for the meeting.</u>

2. You have to finish your homework.
   _____

3. He has to give me more money.
   _____

4. They have to wait for the train.
   _____

5. She has to sell her jewelry.
   _____

6. All the students have to take the test.
   _____

7. You have to read the instructions again.
   _____

8. We have to sleep on the floor.
   _____

9. Aloush has to find a new apartment.
   _____

10. Huda has to ask her mother for money.
    _____

Have to: past tense questions

Questions with *had to* begin with *did*. The subject follows *did*.

Did he *have to* teach on Thursdays?
Did we *have to* do any homework?
Did they *have to* show their ID cards?

Exercise: Change the statements below to questions.

1. I had to be on time for the meeting.
    <u>Did I have to be on time for the meeting?</u>

2. You had to finish your homework.

    _____

3. He had to give me more money.

    _____

4. They had to wait for the train.

    _____

5. She had to sell her jewelry.

    _____

6. All the students had to take the test.

    _____

7. You had to read the instructions again.

    _____

8. We had to sleep on the floor.

    _____

9. Aloush had to find a new apartment.

    _____

10. Huda had to ask her mother for money.

    _____

Have to: future

Will have to expresses need or duty in the future.

He *will have to buy* a bigger house.
We *will have to see* the manager.
They will have to show their ID cards.

Exercise: Change the sentences below to the future with *will have to*.

1. You need to borrow some money.
   <u>You will have to borrow some money.</u>

2. You must be patient with the children.
   _____

3. He must close his bank account.
   _____

4. She must call you back in ten minutes.
   _____

5. We need to change our vacation plans.
   _____

6. It must eat canned food today.
   _____

7. They must find another place to live.
   _____

8. Nabeel needs to buy a new car.
   _____

9. We need to go to the bank tomorrow.
   _____

10. They need to study for the test.
    _____

Have to: future negative

Will not have to expresses the negative of *will have to.*

He *will not have to* buy a bigger house.   He *won't have to* buy a bigger house.
We *will not have to* see the manager.   We *won't have to* see the manager.
They *will not have to* show their ID cards.   They *won't have to* show their ID cards.

Exercise: Change the sentences to negative statements. First use *will not have to.* Then use *won't have to.*

1. You will have to borrow money.
   You will not have to borrow money.
   You won't have to borrow money.

2. You will have to be patient with the children.
   _____
   _____

3. He will have to close his bank account.
   _____
   _____

4. She will have to call you back in ten minutes.
   _____
   _____

5. We will have to change our vacation plans.
   _____
   _____

6. It will have to eat canned food today.
   _____
   _____

7. They will have to find another place to live.
   _____
   _____

8. Nabeel will have to buy a new car.
   _____
   _____

9. We will have to go to the bank tomorrow.
   _____
   _____

Have to: future questions

In questions with *will have to,* the subject follows *will.*

He will have to buy a bigger house.   *Will* he *have to buy* a bigger house?
We will have to see the manager.   *Will* we *have to see* the manager?
They will have to show their ID cards.   *Will* they *have to* show their ID cards?

Exercise: Change the sentences to questions with *will have to?*

1. You will have to take the children with you.
    Will I have to take the children with me?

2. He will have to close his bank account.
    _____

3. She will have to call you back.
    _____

4. We will have to change our vacation plans.
    _____

5. It will have to eat canned food today.
    _____

6. They will have to find another place to live.
    _____

7. Nabeel will have to buy a new car.
    _____

8. We will have to go to the bank tomorrow.
    _____

9. They will have to study for the test.
    _____

10. You will have to borrow money.
    _____

87

Have to: present perfect tense

The perfect form of had to is *have had to*

He has had to buy a bigger house to make room for the new twins.
We *have had to see* the manager about the problem.
They *have had to* show their ID cards every day.

Exercise: Change the verbs in the sentences below to *have had to*.

1. You have to take the children with you.
    You have had to take the children with you.

2. He has to close his bank account.

    _____

3. She has to call you back.

    _____

4. We have to change our vacation plans.

    _____

5. It has to eat canned food today.

    _____

6. They have to find another place to live.

    _____

7. Nabeel has to buy a new car.

    _____

8. We have to go to the bank tomorrow.

    _____

9. They have to study for the test.

    _____

10. You have to borrow money.

    _____

Have to: present perfect negative

The negative form of *have had to* is *have not had to* or *haven't had to.*

He hasn't had to buy a bigger house yet. He is waiting until the new twins arrive.
We haven't had to see the manager about the problem. The supervisor is handling it.
They haven't had to show their ID cards every day. The security guard knows them.

Exercise: Make the sentences below negative.

1. You have had to take the children with you.
    You haven't had to take the children with you.

2. He has had to close his bank account.

3. She has had to call you back.

4. We have had to change our vacation plans.

5. It has had to eat canned food today.

6. They have had to find another place to live.

7. Nabeel has had to buy a new car.

8. We have had to go to the bank.

9. They have had to study for the test.

10. You have had to borrow money.

89

Have to: present perfect questions

In questions with *have had to,* the question begins with *have* or *has,* followed by the subject of the sentence and then *had to.*

Has he **had** to buy a bigger house?
Have they had to see the manager about the problem?
Have they had to show their ID cards everyday?

Exercise: Make questions from the statements below.

1.   You have had to take the children with you.
    Have you had to take the children with you?

2.   He has had to close his bank account.
    _____

3.   She has had to call you back.
    _____

4.   We have had to change our vacation plans.
    _____

5.   It has had to eat canned food today.
    _____

6.   They have had to find another place to live.
    _____

7.   Nabeel has had to buy a new car.
    _____

8.   We have had to go to the bank.
    _____

9.   They have had to study for the test.
    _____

10. You have had to borrow money.
    _____

90

Reflexive Pronouns

Use reflexive pronouns for clarity when the subject and the object are the same person.

I saw *myself* in the mirror.
You saw *yourself* in the mirror.
He saw *himself* in the mirror.
She saw *herself* in the mirror.
It saw *itself* in the mirror.
We saw *ourselves* in the mirror.
You saw *yourselves* in the mirror.
They saw *themselves* in the mirror.

Exercise: Fill in the blank with the appropriate reflexive pronoun.

1.   I shave ___*myself*___ every morning.

2.   The horse hurt _____ when it fell.

3.   You should do the homework _____.

4.   You should all do the homework _____.

5.   They will do the homework _____.

6.   Aloush looked at _____ in the mirror.

7.   Huda burned _____ on the hot stove.

8.   Those children can dress _____.

9.   Our grandfather drives _____ to the clinic.

10.   My grandmother cut _____ while slicing tomatoes.

Reflexive Pronouns: by oneself

Use reflexive pronouns with the preposition *by* to indicate that an action is done *alone*, by a solitary actor.

I went *by myself* to the mountains.
You saw the movie *by yourself*.
He drove *by himself to Jeddah*.
She took a walk in the evening *by herself*.
The cat caught the rat *by itself*.
We exercised *by ourselves every evening*.
You learned English *by yourselves*.
They paid for the house *by themselves*.

Exercise: Rewrite the sentences below. Use *by* and the correct reflexive pronoun.

1. He drove his new car for the first time *alone*.

   He drove his new car for the first time by himself.

2. Huda doesn't like to study *alone*.

   _____

3. The two boys stay at home *alone* while their parents work.

   _____

4. My grandmother lives *alone* in a furnished apartment.

   _____

5. The cat found its way home alone.

   _____

Perfect Modals: Should have

Should have + past participle is used to express opinion or advice after an event (in the past) regarding obligation or necessity. This structure also expresses regret.

Bader <u>should have gone</u> to the doctor.

You <u>should have called</u> me.

She <u>should have bought</u> that car before the price increased.

Exercise: Use a perfect modal (should have + past participle) to change the statements below.

1. I should study an extra hour for the test.

   I should have studied an extra hour for the test.

2. Reem should save her money.

   _____

3. Ahmed should be careful driving at night.

   _____

4. Abdulaziz should eat lunch before he plays football.

   _____

5. We should take lots of water with us to the desert.

   _____

6. They should obey their father.

   _____

Perfect Modals: Ought to have

Ought to have + past participle is used exactly like *should have* to express opinion or advice after an event (in the past) regarding obligation or necessity. Ought to have can also be used to express regret.

Bader <u>*ought to have gone*</u> to the doctor.

You <u>*ought to have called*</u> me.

She <u>*ought to have bought*</u> that car before the price increased.

Exercise: Use a perfect modal (ought to have + past participle) to change the statements below.

1. I should study an extra hour for the test.

   I ought to have studied an extra hour for the test.

2. Reem should save her money.

   _____

3. Ahmed should be careful driving at night.

   _____

4. Abdulaziz should eat lunch before he plays football.

   _____

5. We should take lots of water with us to the desert.

   _____

6. They should obey their father.

   _____

Perfect Modals: Could have

Could have + past participle is used to express a past possibility; an event that might have occurred but didn't.

Salem <u>could have had</u> an accident.

Salwa <u>could have gotten</u> hurt.

Salem didn't have an accident, and Salwa didn't get hurt, but because of some prevailing circumstances it *could have happened, but didn't.*

Exercise: Use a perfect modal (could have + past participle) to change the statements below.

1. We can ride to Dammam with Muneer.
   We could have ridden to Dammam with Muneer.

2. They can leave class early on Wednesday.

   _____

3. Aloush can make a high score on the test.

   _____

4. Nabeel can cook for all of us.

   _____

5. She can go to college.

   _____

6. We can buy the house next door to us.

   _____

95

Perfect Modals: May have

May have + past participle is used to express past possibilities.

Hamed may have forgotten about his appointment.
Muneera may have come late because of car trouble.

When we say *he may have forgotten*, we are not sure that he forgot, but we believe this is a possibility.

Exercise: Use a perfect modal (*may have* + past participle) to express a past possibility based on the statements below.

1. Abdullah was driving a shiny red Toyota.
   _____He may have bought a new car._____

2. Sarah was unable to attend the meeting.
   _____

3. Bader looked sad when he left the classroom after the test.
   _____

4. Ali and Ahmed look exactly alike.
   _____

5. The teacher's face is red.
   _____

6. We have an appointment before the class is finished.
   _____

Perfect Modals: Might have

Might have + past participle, just like may, is used to express past possibilities.

Hamed might have forgotten about his appointment.
Muneera might have come late because of car trouble.

When we say *he might have forgotten*, we are not sure that he forgot, but we believe this is a possibility.

Exercise: Use a perfect modal (*might have* + past participle) to express a past possibility based on the statements below.

1. Abdullah was driving a shiny red Toyota.
   He might have bought a new car.

2. Sarah was unable to attend the meeting.
   _____

3. Bader looked sad when he left the classroom after the test.
   _____

4. Ali and Ahmed look exactly alike.
   _____

5. The teacher's face is red.
   _____

6. We have an appointment before the class is finished.
   _____

Perfect Modals: Must have

Must have + past participle is used to express what we believe is true.

He must have forgotten.
Miriam must have come late.

When we say *he must have forgotten*, we are not sure that he forgot, but we believe this to be true

Exercise: Use a perfect modal (*must have* + past participle) to make an assumption about the statements below.

1. Abdullah was driving really fast.
   <u>He must have been in a hurry.</u>

2. Sarah bought several hamburgers.
   _____

3. Bader stayed up late last night with his English books.
   _____

4. Ali and Ahmed arrived in the same car.
   _____

5. The teacher is smiling today.
   _____

6. We don't have our books with us.
   _____

Continuous Modals

Three commonly used *continuous modals* are:

> may be + <u>present participle (V+ing)</u>
> might be + <u>present participle (V+ing)</u>
> could be + <u>present participle (V+ing)</u>

These structures are interchangeable, and they are generally used to indicate the possibility that something is happening *at the moment* of speaking.

Example: I'm expecting an important call from my boss. Please get off the phone.

> He might be trying to call me right now.

Exercise: Use a continuous modal form to answer the question.

1. I don't think Aloush is serious about his two-headed cow.

   Maybe he is joking.

2. What do you think Jaber is doing right now?

   _____

3. Why do you think Khalid is late?

   _____

4. Whose car is Mansoor driving?

   _____

5. Where is Nasser working now?

   _____

Be supposed to

Be supposed to expresses the idea that an event or a behavior is expected to happen.

The test is supposed to begin at nine o'clock in the morning.
The students are supposed to be silent during the test.

Exercise: Answer the questions with *be supposed to.*

1. What are students supposed to do when the teacher is speaking?

   Students are supposed to listen to the teacher.

2. Who is supposed to take care of the children when they are young?

   _____

3. Where are you supposed to take your medical prescription?

   _____

4. What are you supposed to do to your car when it is dirty?

   _____

5. Where am I supposed to go if I have a toothache?

   _____

6. What am I supposed to buy in order to fly on an airplane?

   _____